PUBLISHED
to Examine
the Historical,
Political and
Religious Background
of the 1644 and 1689
Baptist
Confessions of Faith

By
Richard P. Belcher
and
Anthony Mattia

A Discussion of the
Seventeenth Century
Particular Baptist Confessions of Faith

CONTENTS

Crowne Publications, Inc.
P.O. Box 688
Southbridge, MA 01550

ISBN 0-925703-23-0

Printed in the United States of America

INTRODUCTION

THE PROBLEM

In 1644 seven Baptist congregations in London published a confession that has come to be known as the First
London Confession of Faith. A second edition of this confession appeared in 1646. Most recently this 1646 edition has
been reprinted and made available to Baptists of the twentieth century.[1] Included in this 1981 reprint is an appendix
to the 1646 edition which was written by Benjamin Cox, a
London preacher of that day.

The purpose stated for bringing this seventeenth century confession into print once again is a claim that the
better-known and more popular Baptist confession of 1689
(the Second London Confession) does not reflect the true and
earliest particular Baptist thought in the area of the law of
God. A further claim is that the 1689 confession was forced
on Baptists through political and religious coercion. These
are serious charges, and if they are true they have far-reaching consequences for particular Baptists of our day who have
assumed that the 1689 confession was a continuation of
earlier particular Baptist thought.

Before moving on to test these claims, it will be necessary
to be sure they are correctly understood. That will be ac-

complished by allowing the advocates of the supremacy of the 1646 confession to state their case.

The Issue of the Law

In the 'Contemporary Preface to the 1646 Confession' Gary Long states the argument concerning the contradictory views of the law of the 1646 and the 1689 confessions. He says:

> Why republish the 1646 edition of the First London Confession of Faith—the London Baptist Confession of 1644—with an appendix to it also written in 1646? Why not use the Second London Confession—the London Baptist Confession of Faith of 1689—a Baptist modification of the Westminster Confession of Faith of 1646? Both of these latter Confessions are currently in print and readily available. The principle reason lies in the following explanation. In examining the Westminster Confession of 1646 (including its larger Catechism) and the Second London Confession of 1689, one will find stress placed upon the law of God summarily comprehended in the Mosaic decalogue as a rule of life for the believer. Conversely, the stress of the First London Confession of 1644, and its second edition in 1646, is upon the New Covenant commands, or law of Christ. In sum, although all of these confessions are in basic agreement concerning the abiding nature of God's eternal moral law, there is a distinctive New Covenant emphasis concerning biblical law in the 1644 and 1646 editions of the First London Confession that is distinctly lacking in the Old Covenant emphasis of the Westminster and Second London Confessions. This distinction in the Confessions has important theological implications in understanding both the role of the Biblical law as God's ethical standard or rule for the believer's life under the New Covenant, and for understanding the relationship of the law of God to the

gospel of Jesus Christ. Hence the contemporary reason for the republishing of the First London Confession.[2]

Note carefully the following points stressed by Long in his above statement:

1. In both the 1644 and the 1689 confessions there is basic agreement concerning the abiding nature of God's eternal moral law.

2. In the 1689 confession stress is placed on the law of God as comprehended in a summary manner in the Mosaic decalogue and such is to be the rule of life for the believer.

3. In the 1644 (and 1646) confessions there is to be found a distinctive New Covenant emphasis that is lacking in the 1689 confession.

4. The distinction in the emphasis of these confessions concerning the law of God (the 1689 emphasized the Old Covenant statement of the law as the believer's rule of life, while the 1644 stresses the New Covenant as the believer's rule of life) is the reason for the republishing of the 1646 confession.

On the back cover of the same document we have been discussing (the republished 1646 confession), the argument is presented once again in the following statement:

There is a distinctive New Covenant emphasis concerning Biblical Law in the 1644 and 1646 editions of the First London Confession that is regretfully lacking in the Old Covenant emphasis of the Westminster and Second London Confessions. This difference has far-reaching theological implications.[3]

Thus it has been clearly shown that some are advocating today that there exists a difference in emphasis on the law of God in the two major particular Baptist confessions of faith of the seventeenth century. It is being claimed that the earliest confession of 1644 and its editions stress the New Covenant as the rule of life of the believer rather than the Old Covenant, while the later confession of 1689 stressed only the Old Covenant.

The Issue of Coercion in 1689

The second reason being given for the superiority of the 1646 confession, and hence its present-day republication, is that the 1689 confession does not truly reflect Baptist thought due to political persecution and pressure. Baptists, to some extent, it is being claimed, were coerced to draw up a confession that was almost identical to the Westminster Confession of Faith. Long states the argument for us again as follows:

> The significance of Lumpkin's observation lies in the fact that the Second London Confession—the London Confession adopted in 1689—was tailored to the Westminster Confession of Faith of 1646 under the conditions of persecution from the State-Church of England—circumstances which caused it to read almost identical to the Westminster Confession on the law of God and most other areas, except on church government and civil magistrates. Hence, the historical reason for republishing the First London Baptist Confession, namely, to restate the Particular Baptist confessional position, especially on the law of God, before being heavily influenced by the Westminster Confession which was formulated at an assembly summoned by the state, and in which Particular Baptists were not permitted to attend.[4]

To summarize briefly the above statement by Long for the sake of clearly grasping his argument, note the following points:

1. The confession of 1689 (the Second London Confession) was almost identical to the Westminster Confession of 1646, including its view of the law of God.

2. The confession of 1689 possessed this great similarity to the Westminster Confession of 1646 because of persecution from the State-Church of England.

3. The confession of 1644 (the First London Confession) is being republished to restate the Particular Baptist confessional view, primarily on the subject of the law of God.

To summarize the historical development of the law of God in the Baptist confessions, as also given in Long's statement here, note again the following:

1. Particular Baptists set forth their view of the law of God *in the confession of 1644* (the Fist London Confession), and their view in that confession stressed the New Covenant rather than the Old Covenant as the rule of life for the believer.

2. Particular Baptists were not involved in the formulation of *the Westminster Confession of 1646*, as it was formulated at a state-called assembly from which Particular Baptists were excluded. This confession set forth the Old Covenant as the rule of the believer's life rather than the New Covenant.

3. Particular Baptists adopted *the confession of 1689* (the Second London Confession, which was a restatement, for the most part, of the Westminster Confession, containing its emphasis on the Old Covenant as the rule of the believer's life) only out of coercion and persecution from the state church of England.

4. Hence, the conclusion of some today that *the confession of 1644* is the true Particular Baptist confession, and gives the true Particular Baptist view of the law of God.

We now turn to test these two claims of Long and others today concerning the Baptist confessions of the seventeenth century. Was the 1689 confession adopted because of political and religious coercion? Does the 1646 confession present a different view of the law than the 1689 confession? Further research into these two confessions and their backgrounds is necessary before one can determine the issue. We shall begin with the 1644 confession, then move to consider in some depth the 1689 confession.

CHAPTER 1

THE FIRST LONDON CONFESSION

By the year 1644 there existed seven particular Baptist churches in London.[1] The community in which they lived seriously misunderstood their doctrinal viewpoint, and thus they were accused of all kinds of errors and supposed heresies. There were accused of being Anabaptists, and thus looked upon as a sect that was out of step completely with the existing society. Many did not distinguish them from the General Baptists, and in light of the fact that England at this time was strongly Calvinistic, they were not enhanced in the eyes of the people about them.

These conditions led to the conviction that a particular Baptist confession of faith was not only in order but greatly needed. Calvinistic Baptists could not go on being mistaken for Anabaptists and Arminians. It was determined that their best defense against the false accusations and unfounded assumptions about their churches was to draw up and adopt a confession of faith. As such a confession was published, it would then be clear to all what they believed and practiced. Fifteen men representing only the seven churches in London signed the new confession in 1644 which has come to be known as the First London Confession of Faith. Whitley says that these fifteen men had already 'linked their churches together.'[2] He says further that each one of these men who can be historically identified and traced was 'an ardent evangelist.'[3] Thus the First London Confession came into existence in 1644 and was signed by fifteen men who represented seven churches in the city of London.

The Sources of the First London Confession

It may be commonly assumed that the First London Confession was drawn up independently by the fifteen representatives of the seven churches which signed the 1644 edition. Nothing is said of any sources in most discussions of the 1644 or 1646 editions of this seventeenth century document. Many assume these early Calvinistic Baptists were original in their confessional statements and doctrinal formulations. It is often pointed out by the present day advocates of the First London Confession that the Second London Confession of 1689 had the Westminster confession for its basic source; but no one we have read or talked with who supports the First London Confession has raised the question of the sources of this statement of faith.

The fact of the matter is that the First London Confession used earlier non-Baptist confessions as its source for many of its articles of faith. The two confessions used most extensively were dated in 1596[4] and 1616. The second was known as the Aberdeen Confession.[5] Another source of the 1644 confession was a document known as the 'Points of Difference' between the Congregationalists and the Church of England which was submitted to James I at his succession to the throne in 1603.[6] The articles taken from this document were 5-7. It is a startling fact, as McGlothlin states it, that thirty-two out of fifty-three articles were derived from Congregational documents.[7] The Congregational Confession of 1596 only had forty-five articles to begin with. Those articles which were used from the Congregational Confession were:

1-9; 24-26; 34; 36; 38; and 41-44. Concerning the closeness of the 1644 Baptist confession to the 1596 Congregational confession, McGlothlin states further:

> None of these articles were verbatim repetitions of those found in the Congregational documents but most of the changes in the order of words, in spelling and capitalization, the substitution of synonymous terms, etc. Many of these changes are made on no recognizable principle, but appear as if they were the result of an effort to reproduce the articles from memory. In about twenty instances the articles were taken over almost verbatim, which in the remaining cases there were more or less extensive and important changes made by the omission or addition of phrases, clauses or sentences. In some cases there were both omissions and additions to the same article.[8]

McGlothlin also comments on several other aspects of the 1644 confession. First, there is a definite attempt '...to simplify the confession by the omissions of obtuse theological terms, and theological ideas not well authenticated in Scripture.'[9] In the article on the Trinity the statement that there are 'three distinct persons coeternal, coequal and coessential, being every one of them one and the same God,' is changed to read "In this God-head, there is the Father, the Son and the Spirit, being every one of them one and the same God,' etc.

Second, McGlothlin contends that in the 1644 confession 'There is a very clear and definite softening of the Calvinism of the Congregational Confession in article 3.'[10] A comparison of the statements of the two confessions on the doctrine of election reveals the following:

1596 Congregational Confession	1644 Baptist Confession
And touching his cheefest Creatures that hath in Christ before the foundation of the world, according to the good pleasure of his vvill, ordeyned some men and Angells, to eternall lyfe to bee accomplished through Jesus Christ, to the prayse of the glorie of his grace. And on thother hand hath likevvise before of old according to his just purpose ordeyned other both Angells and men, to eternall condemnation, to be accomplished through their own corruption to the prayse of his justice.[11]	And touching his creature man, God had in Christ before the foundation of the world, according to the good pleasure of His will foreordained some men to eternall life through Jesus Christ, to the praise and glory of his grace, leaving the rest in their sinne to their just condemnation, to the praise of his justice.[11]

Perhaps the above is part of the reason that McGlothlin concluded in another place that the 1644 Baptist confession on examination will be seen not to have been very carefully drawn, and was only moderately Calvinistic.[12]

None of the above facts concerning the sources of the 1644 confession are stated to disqualify it as an adequate statement of the Particular Baptist convictions of that day. Rather these facts are stated to show that the 1644 confession had non-Baptist sources as did the 1689 confession. In simple words the 1689 confession cannot be discredited solely on the ground that it had a non-Baptist source, because the 1644 confession had the same. A confession must not be judged on the basis of its source alone, but more primarily on its faithfulness or unfaithfulness to Scripture.

Further, the conviction of McGlothlin that the 1644 confession simplifies the theological language and even softens the Calvinism does not discredit it as a reliable statement of Particular Baptist thought. One could argue this may evidence an attempt to be practical and clearly communicative to anyone of that day who might wish to understand what Baptists believed. In fact, it may be the result of the attempt to fulfill the statement on the cover page which reads:

> A Confession Of Faith Of Seven Congregations Or Churches Of Christ In London, Which Are Commonly (But Unjustly) Called Anabaptists Published For The Vindication Of The Truth And Information Of The Ignorant; Likewise For The Pulpit And Print Unjustly Cast Upon Them.[13]

The conclusion must be that non-Baptist sources heavily influenced both the 1644 and the 1689 confessions, and therefore any argument that would disqualify either of these confessions based on source alone would also disqualify the other. However, religious and political circumstances surrounding the sources and their use would be another question.

The Revision of the First London Confession

The 1644 confession known as the First London Confession did not meet with favorable acceptance from everyone. Severe criticism of it surfaced primarily from a Dr. Daniel Featley who preached in the state church in London. He had been a member of the Westminster Assembly, but under the suspicion and accusation of disloyalty was imprisoned by the Parliamentary authorities. It was while he was in prison that the 1644 Baptist confession was printed. Featley wrote a book while in prison with the last chapter devoted to the criticism of the new confession, as well as the Baptists who had printed it. He published his book in 1645 and dedicated the book to Parliament.

Featley leveled several false accusations against these particular Baptists who were behind the 1644 confession. He was convinced that they were Arminian and perhaps even

Pelagian in theology.[14] He associated them with the
Anabaptists and the earlier English Baptists. Actually, these
Baptists were Calvinistic, as the confession clearly shows.
Featley also accused them of denying that the Christian could
serve as a civil magistrate or take an oath.[15] Again, he
confused them with the Anabaptists. In all, Featley criticized
six of the fifty-three articles in the 1644 confession.

The result of Featley's criticism was the 1646 edition, as
the Baptists felt a need to reply to his accusations. Mc-
Glothlin writes concerning the revised London Confession
of 1646 (the one recently published by Backus Publications):

> Accordingly it was subjected to a careful revision,
> removing obscurities an infelicities of language, reclas-
> sifying the material and rearranging the articles, and
> removing as far as possible the language objected to by
> Featley in the six articles criticized by him. Indeed, they
> went too far in this latter respect as seriously to weaken
> the distinctive Baptist character of some of the articles.
> This revised edition was then dedicated to Parliament,
> as Featley's attack had been in a brief but rigorous
> epistle.[16]

Not only did these Baptists revise their confession to satisfy
Dr. Featley, but they also dedicated the new edition to Par-
liament as Featley had dedicated his attack against them.
That dedication begins as follows:

> To the Right Honorable the Lords, Knights, Citizens
> and Burgesses in Parliament Assemblies. Right
> Honorable and Most Noble Patriots, In as much as
> there hath been a book (Featley's) lately presented unto
> you, in whose Dedicatory Epistle there are many
> heinous accusations unjustly and falsely laid against
> us, we conceived it necessary to make some declaration
> of our innocency, and (to that end) humbly to present
> into your view this our Confession of Faith.[17]

McGlothlin criticizes Baptists at this point for bending their doctrine in the 1646 revision due to Featley's criticism.[18] The following comparisons will allow the reader to judge McGlothlin's assessment of the matter (the part omitted in the 1646 confession is in bold type in the 1644).

1644	1646
Article XXXVIII	Article XXXVIII
*That the due maintenance of the Officers aforesaid, should be the free and voluntary communication of the Church, that according to Christ's Ordinance, they that preach the Gospel, should live on the Gospel **and not by constraint to be compelled from the people by a forced Law.***	*The ministers of Christ ought to have whatsoever they shall need, supplied freely by the church, that according to Christ's ordinance, they that preach the Gospel, shall live of the Gospel by the law of Christ.*

McGlothlin contends that 'The Baptist point of religious freedom and separation between church and state is so far blunted (in the 1646 confession) that Dr. Featley himself could have signed it without hesitation or reservation. The Baptists could maintain their position under this article, but no longer by it.'[19]

1644	1646
Article XXXIX	Article XXXIX
*That Baptisme is an Ordinance of the New Testament given by Christ, to be dispensed **onely** upon persons professing faith, or that are Disciples or taught, who upon a profession of faith, ought to be baptized.*	*Baptism is an ordinance of the New Testament, given by Christ to be dispensed upon persons professing faith, or that are made disciples; who upon profession of faith, ought to be baptized, and after to partake of the Lord's Supper.*

Of the dropping of the word only in the 1646 confession, McGlothlin says 'Again the point of the Baptist contention is gone and their critic could sign the revised article without constraint of conscience. One can here scarcely defend them against the charge of unfaithfulness to their convictions.'[20]

1644	1646
Article XL	Article XL
*The way and manner of the dispensing of this Ordinance **the Scripture holds out to be** dipping or plunging the whole body under the water: it being a signe, must answer the thing signified, which are these, etc.*	*That the way and manner of dispensing this ordinance, is dipping or plunging the body under water; it being a sign, must answer the things signified, which is, etc.*

McGlothlin terms the exclusion of the reference to Scripture as the authority of baptism as surprising.[21] He indicates this omission was due to Featley's assertion '...that Scriptures nowhere, either by precept or example, prescribe immersion as the only mode of baptism... They cling to their mode, but give up or at least do not any longer assert it on Scripture authority.'[22]

Though there were other changes, one more will be mentioned. Featley had criticized the 1644 confession and Baptists regarding their view of the Christian serving as a civil magistrate. He was convinced they would not allow a Christian to serve in that place of authority nor take an oath. Though the 1644 confession had mentioned the office of the magistrate, it had made no statement either way concerning a believer filling it. Featley took this omission as evidence they were opposed to the believer serving in such a role. The result of Featley's criticism was an added article in the 1646 confession which read as follows:

> It is lawfull for a Christian to be a magistrate or Civill Officer; and also it is lawfull to take an Oath, so it be in truth, and in judgment, and in righteousness, for confirmation of truth, and ending of all strife; and that by rash and vaine Oaths the Lord is provoked, and this Land mournes.[23]

McGlothlin summarized the influence of Featley on the revisions in the 1646 confession as follows:

> From this it will be seen that Featley's book made a profound impression on the Baptists—not on their views, but on the statement of those views. They felt the necessity of removing every possible cause of offense in the statement of those views, and in three instances they go to the danger line by way of concession, if not beyond it. It only shows how sensitive they were to the dangers that beset them.[24]

Thus it is quite clear and beyond dispute that Baptists in the middle of the fourth decade of the seventeenth century bowed to the religious and political pressures of their times as they faced some severe criticism to their confession of 1644. The result was the 1646 revised confession, which according to McGlothlin, was a serious weakening of the distinctive Baptist character of some of the articles.[25] He even contends some articles were so blunted that Featley himself could have signed them without reservation or hesitation or constraint of conscience. As noted above also, McGlothlin says there is no way one could defend them against the charge of unfaithfulness to their convictions.

Yet the group of Baptists today who are advocating the supremacy of the 1646 confession over the 1689 confession are saying nothing of these alleged compromises on Baptist distinctives found in the former. The 'Contemporary Preface' by Gary Long in the Backus edition of the 1646 confession doesn't even hint at these concessions.[26] Rather, these modern proponents of the 1646 statement of Baptist faith accuse the 1689 confession of bowing to religious and political pressure on the matter of the law. One can hardly be honest and consistent when he rejects one confession on the alleged ground it has compromised Baptist distinctives because of religious and political pressures of the day, while accepting and promoting another confession of faith which clearly does the same.

In all fairness, it must be pointed out before closing this section, there were changes in the second edition (1646) which strengthened the Calvinism. There was the denial of free will, the denial of falling from grace, the denial of communalism, a stronger statement on election, and a statement on original sin.[27] But these issues were not those contested by Featley nor others of the state church. In fact these changes would have been welcomed by the state church, and would have in no way been offensive to them. One could argue that this was done consciously to bring the favor of the state church, as were the previously mentioned statements modified which compromised Baptist distinctives.

The Benjamin Cox Appendix

Late in 1646, after the publication of the 1646 revised edition, there appeared a twenty-two article booklet entitled 'An Appendix to the Confession of Faith.' It was authored by Benjamin Cox, an Oxford graduate and one of the signers of the 1646 revision. Some feel that Cox had probably assisted in the revision. This raises the question why the appendix was needed if Cox had been on the revision committee? Apparently, Cox felt the 1646 confession did not explain some particulars with his desired clarity, and therefore he was compelled to address himself to some further matters. The title page reads 'An Appendix To A Confession Of Faith or A More Full Declaration of the Faith and Judgment of Baptized Believers Occasioned by the Inquiry of Some Wo-affected and Godly Persons in the Country.'[28] The title page further states it was 'Published for the further clearing of Truth, and discovery of their mistake who have imagined a dissent in fundamentals when there is none.'[29]

This appendix, as far as it is known, was never published at that time with the confession.[30] The Backus' publication of the confession and appendix seems to be the first publication of the two together. It must be remembered that Cox's appendix is not the confession. Further, no one else signed his publication, although he claimed to speak for the seven churches. McGlothlin says that Cox's articles '...stiffen the Calvinism, declare belief in eternal punishment, define the Christian's relation to the law and to good works more clearly, and express some other points a little more fully than the Confession.'[31]

This need of an appendix and the recognition of the appendix by the modern advocates of the supremacy of the 1646 revised edition, raises some interesting questions. How can one criticize the signers of the Second London Confession of 1689 as they, like Cox, stressed their agreement with the 1644 confession, yet at the same time felt a need to enlarge upon it and clarify it? Further, if Cox felt a need to clarify the 1646 confession on the subject of the law, how can we criticize the men of 1689 for further attempting to clarify the same subject (if they so attempted to do this)? Fairness and honesty demand we give the 1689 men the same privilege we would give to Cox.

Other Revisions

A third edition to the First London Confession appeared in 1651, followed by a fourth edition in 1652. Changes were minor and dealt mainly with the rising force of quakerism. Whitley comments on these two editions as he says, 'The editions of 1651 and 1652 show that they had slightly modified their views again and again; while an introductory note denies that they had been misled by the Quakers...'[32] Whitley notes further that another edition was published 'by Londoners in the army at Leith, to explain Baptists to Scotland, and especially to dissociate from the Quakers.'[33] He adds that Thomas Collier drew up another confession which was approved in 1656 by the Western Association. He says of this confession that it '...referred to and agreed generally with the London Confession, but they did not exalt it into a touchstone.'[34]

Finally, Whitley quotes their reasons for these revisions as follows:

> ...to speak the truth for us, and so make our innocency to appeare; desiring that the same light may guide others also to the same way of truth.[35]

But even further, they showed an openness to further development in their theological understanding as they said:

> Also we confesse that we know but in part, and that we are ignorant of many things which we desire and seek to know; and if any shall doe us that friendly part to show us from the Word of God that we see not, we shall have cause to be thankfull to God and them.[36]

The New Covenant Emphasis of
The First London Confession

We now face a question which was raised by Gary Long in the Backus publication of the 1646 First London Confession.[37] His contention in the preface to that work is that the First London Confession stresses the New Covenant commands of Christ as the rule for the life of the believer, while the Second London Confession emphasizes the Mosaic decalogue as the believer's standard of life. The question regarding the viewpoint of the First London Confession will now be considered, while the conviction of the Second London Confession will be discussed in chapter two.

The Statements of the Confession
Concerning the New Covenant

The easiest way to determine the issue for the reader's benefit will be to quote each section from the First London Confession (the revised edition of 1646) which mentions the New Covenant or the law of Christ. Note these following statements (bold letters are added so the reader may clearly and quickly identify the New Covenant words):

Article X

*Jesus Christ is made the mediator of the **new and everlasting covenant** of grace between God and man, ever to be perfectly and fully the prophet, priest, and king of the Church of God forevermore.*[38]

Article XXIX

*All believers are a holy and sanctified people, and that sanctification is a spiritual grace of the **new covenant**, and an effect of the love of God manifested in the soul, whereby* *the believer presseth after a heavenly and evangelical obedience to all the commands, which Christ as head and king in His **new covenant** hath presented to them.*[39]

Article XXX

*All believers through the knowledge of that justification of life given by the Father and brought forth by the blood of Christ have as their great privilege of that **new covenant**, peace with God, reconciliation, whereby they that were afar off are made nigh by that blood, and have peace passing all understanding; yea, joy in God through our Lord Jesus Christ, by whom we have received the atonement.*[40]

Article XXXVIII

The ministers of Christ ought to have whatsoever they shall need, supplied freely by the church, that according to Christ's ordinance they that preach the Gospel should live of the gospel by the law of Christ.[41]

Article XLVIII

*...And concerning the worship of God; there is but **one lawgiver**, which is able to save and destroy, **James 4:12; which is Jesus Christ**, who hath given laws and rules sufficient in His word for his worship; and for any to make more, were to charge Christ with want of wisdom, of faithfulness, or both, in not making laws enough, or not good enough for His house: Surely it is our wisdom, duty, and privilege, **to observe Christ's laws only, Ps. 2:6, 9, 10, 12.***[42]

The Conclusion

*...but if any man shall impose upon us anything that we see not to be **commanded by our Lord Jesus Christ**, we should*

in His strength rather embrace all reproaches and tortures of men,...[43]

The previous quotations are all of the references from the 1646 confession concerning the commands or laws of Christ. The question is, do these statements as a whole, or does any one of these statements singularly convince the reader that these early particular Baptists rejected the law of Moses as the rule of life for the believer in preference to the exclusive use of Christ's New Covenant commands as the standard of obedience? Considering the articles one at a time, what does one have to conclude?

Article X does not establish their argument. It merely refers to Christ as the mediator of the new and everlasting covenant.

Article XXIX does not establish the argument either. It merely states that sanctification is a spiritual grace of the new covenant, and that it results in the believer pressing towards an obedience to all of Christ's commands. It does not disassociate the Old Testament decalogue from those commands. It does not state that the Sermon on the Mount annuls or abrogates the Old Testament decalogue.

Article XXX does not establish the case either. It doesn't even mention the decalogue, but rather states that believers possess peace with God, reconciliation, etc., as their privilege in the new covenant.

Article XXXVIII speaks not of the decalogue but of the preacher of the gospel living of the gospel by the law of Christ.

Article XLVIII's note must be seen in its context to be correctly understood. The article speaks of the civil magistracy, but disallows that authority to have any relation or reign in the area of the worship of God. The note then states that there is one lawgiver in that spiritual realm, and that lawgiver is Jesus Christ. He has given us in His Word all the rules we need for His worship. In this realm the believer is under the authority of Christ and not the authority of the civil magistrate. Notice the statement says He has given laws and rules in His Word (not just the New Testament) for His worship. Also notice the Scriptural references concerning observing Christ's laws are from the Old Testament, not just the New Testament.

The conclusion does not establish the argument either. That section sets forth their loyalty to Christ, their desire to live at peace with all men, and their openness to listen to the word of God (not just the New Testament) if they are wrong. But this section also clearly lets all men know that if someone seeks to impose upon them other than the authority of Christ, they shall be willing to suffer all persecution before doing anything against the truth of God. In this statement there is nothing that denies the authority of the Old Testament or the decalogue in the Old Testament.

Therefore the conclusion is that there is no clear statement or statements in the 1646 confession that sets forth the New Covenant commands of Christ as the rule for the life of the believer in opposition to the Old Testament decalogue.

The Statements of the Confession
Concerning the Word of God

Other statements of the confession must be considered when seeking to determine whether there exists in it a New Covenant emphasis, or a rejection of the decalogue as the rule of the life of the believer. What does this 1646 confession say about the rest of the Bible? Does it view all Scripture as authoritative for the believer, or just the New Testament? To pick out a few articles that mention the New Covenant while ignoring other statements which might speak of the authority of the entire Scripture is neither fair nor honest. Note the following articles and sections of articles which beyond doubt see all Scripture as the authority of the believer (again the bold lettering is added).

Article VIII

*The **rule** of this knowledge, faith, and obedience, concerning the worship of God, in which is contained **the whole duty of man,** is (not men's laws, or unwritten traditions, but) **only the Word of God contained in the holy Scriptures;** in which is plainly recorded whatsoever is needful for us to know, believe, and **practice; which are the only rule of holiness and obedience for all saints, at all times, in all places to be observed.**[44]*

Article XLV

*Also such to whom God hath given gifts in the church, may and ought to prophecy according to the proportion of faith, and to **teach publicly the Word of God for the edification, exhortation, and comfort of the church.**[45]*

Article XLIX

*But in case we find not the magistrate to favor us herein; yet we dare not suspend our practice, because we believe we ought to go in obedience to Christ, in professing **the faith which was once delivered to the saints, which faith is declared in Scriptures, and this is our witness to the truth of the Old and New Testament unto the death.**[46]*

These statements are clear in themselves, but just in case the reader missed the point, the following comments will help to spell out the arguments.

Article VIII declares indisputably that these particular Baptists believed the Word of God in holy Scripture (Old Testament and New Testament as well) was the rule which contains the whole duty of man. These holy Scriptures are the only rule of holiness and obedience for all saints in all places *at all times*. Who can dispute the plainness of this statement! How could one possibly argue that this confession rejects the decalogue as a rule of life for the believer?

Article XLV declares that the men God has gifted are to preach publicly the Word of God (no distinction is made between the Old and New Testaments). Part of this preaching of the Word of God includes exhortation—the challenge to obedience. If only the commands of Christ are the rule of the believer's life for the particular Baptists of the seventeenth century, why didn't they say so here?

Article XLIX states clearly these men stand for the faith once delivered to the saints. That faith has been declared in Scripture (not just the New Testament) and it is clearly declared that the authors of this confession will stand for all the Scripture (Old and New Testament is spelled out) even to death.

Again, the conclusion when one looks at the entire confession is that there is no ground for the claim that the First London Confession has a New Covenant emphasis, with the commands of Christ placed above the decalogue to the absolute enthronement of the former and the exclusion of the latter. No, rather the entire Word of God is every believer's authority at all times.

The Judgment of Other Historians

Another question is always helpful when one is seeking to unravel and understand an historical event and document. Am I understanding this in agreement with the best historians of the past and the present? This is not always conclusive but it can be a barricade to the total misreading of the document or situation. One must also admit that there are times even when the best historians disagree and take opposite positions. Again, it is not uncommon for one historian, after studying the historical documents, and from his vast knowledge of the background of the day, to set himself in opposition to the other historians of the past and present.

As one applies the test of the understanding of the best Baptist historians to this question of the New Covenant emphasis in the 1646 confession, it has to be admitted that their testimony is undeniably in agreement against such a view. The bibliography of this present work lists many of those great Baptist historians as sources, but not *one* of them has even suggested such a possibility as is advocated by the preface in the Backus edition. Besides these men listed in the bibliography, other great Baptist historians were read in the research of the subject, but again not one of them saw such a New Covenant emphasis in the First London Confession. Remember, some of these men were English Baptist historians, who have or had further sources, no doubt, not available to us. But again, not one of them would be in agreement with the new interpretation of the confession.

In a discussion with Dr. William Lumpkin (see bibliography), he stated his conviction that there is no difference of belief between the 1646 and 1689 confessions as far as essential doctrines are concerned.[47] He saw no distinct New Covenant emphasis in the earlier confession, and he felt that this was being read into the document. When told specifically which articles are said to contain the New Covenant teachings, he failed to see the significance or possibility of building such a theological concept from these references. Thus the New Covenant idea completely fails the Baptist historian test.

A Final Argument

The claims that some have made in our day that the First London Confession has a stress on New Covenant commands, we have seen, does not stand up before the historical evidence. Now one final argument against those claims is added. The previous evidence has been strong and now this final piece of argumentation should clinch the case against those who are misinterpreting and misrepresenting the 1646 confession.

First, the reader is asked to recall two facts of history that have been mentioned or at least alluded to in the course of previous discussion. Does the reader remember the reason given for the publication of the First London Confession? That reason was clearly and conspicuously recorded on the front cover or title page of both the first and second edition. The title page of the 1644 edition has the following as its identifying banner:

The
CONFESSION
OF FAITH
of those Churches which are
commonly (though falsely) called
ANABAPTISTS[48]

The cover of the Backus publication edition (and one can suppose it is the cover or title page of that original second edition) reads as follows:

A
CONFESSION OF FAITH
of seven congregations or churches of
Christ in London, which are commonly
(but unjustly) called Anabaptists[49]

It is to be noted that reference is made to Anabaptists in both of the above titles. However, it is not in order to align themselves with that group, but to declare emphatically that particular Baptists are not to be confused with the Anabaptists of the past or present. Therefore these titles are evidence that the First London Confession was a reactionary work in some sense to the strong accusations that were being hurled at them which equated them with Anabaptists. Since that is the case, one can expect the confession to carefully and purposefully avoid any language that could be interpreted as promoting any Anabaptist areas of theology.

It may come as a shock to some, but the view being embraced and promoted today which says the First London Confession has a New Covenant emphasis which eliminates the decalogue as the rule of life for the believer, is to say this confession stated an Anabaptist view of the Law. This is a preposterous interpretation of the confession in light of the fact that its explicit purpose was to separate particular Baptist theology from Anabaptist theology.

In case the reader asks for some documentation which would show that the Anabaptists possessed an emphasis on the New Covenant commands as superior to and a replacement of the Old Testament decalogue, the following evidence is offered. Klassen says that one of the two major hermeneutical issues of the Reformation was the relationship of the Old and New Covenants.[50] He notes further in the same context that this issue rose at every major disputation between Reformed thought and Anabaptist thought. He argues also that Anabaptists provoked the discussion to a greater extent than is usually admitted.

Estep in his important and authoritative work on Anabaptists discussed Pilgrim Marpeck's view of Scripture.[51] Marpeck was committed to the Bible as the Word of God, Estep says, but for him there was an absolute distinction between the Old and New Testaments. For him and other Anabaptists, such as the Swiss Brethren, the Hutterites, and Mennonites, the New Testament alone was the rule of faith and practice. Finally, Estep notes that Marpeck's view of Scripture and revelation was dependent on Paul's treatment of the relation between the two covenants in Galatians.

Thus the argument is established. The First London Confession stresses a desire to establish a strong distinction between Anabaptists and particular Baptists. Anabaptists held to an antithesis between the Old and New Testaments, with a strong emphasis on the New Covenant commands as opposed to the Old Testament commands. Therefore, we say again that it is preposterous to interpret the First London Confession as setting forth an Anabaptist view of the Old and New Covenants.

But the argument is strengthened by remembering a second fact from our earlier discussion. Remember Featley's attack? He was the State preacher who was convinced these particular Baptists were Anabaptists. In one of the later chapters of a book, he assailed the First London Confession at the points which he was convinced set forth Anabaptist theology. So sensitive were these English particular Baptists about being called Anabaptist by Featley, that they modified their confession at the points of his attack. Interestingly enough, Featley did not interpret the confession at any place to set forth an Anabaptist view of the Old and New Covenants as some moderns are doing today. Surely he is a better guide for interpreting these controversial statements than someone of modern times who is far-removed from the historical setting and events.

Summary

As this chapter concludes, it will be helpful for the reader to see the points of argument which have been established concerning the controversy of our day over the First London Confession and the Second London Confession.

First, the First London Confession had for its sources non-Baptist documents, primarily two non-Baptist confessions dated 1596 and 1616. Therefore one cannot fault nor reject the Second London Confession simply on the ground that it had for its source the non-Baptist Westminster Confession of Faith.

Second, the 1646 edition (second edition) of the First London Confession, which some modern Baptists are promoting as a more Baptistic confession than the Second London Confession, actually modified and perhaps even watered down some of the strong Baptist concepts which had been included in the first edition. Therefore, one can hardly argue that this confession is the purest possible representation of the Baptist faith for that day.

Third, the Appendix by Benjamin Cox, as far as it is known, was never published with the confession until the Backus publication of the two in 1981. Therefore, it cannot be taken as the authoritative statement of particular Baptists of that day, but only as the convictions of one man.

Fourth, the particular Baptists of the seventeenth century never claimed any of their confessions to be the final word on doctrinal matters, because other editions followed.

Fifth, (and perhaps the most important point of the chapter) it is a false and improper interpretation of the First London Confession to conclude that it has a stress on the New Covenant commands of Christ as the only rule of the believer's life. The statements of the confession do not say this; further, other statements of the confession contradict this idea; the judgment of the best Baptist historians negate this idea; and finally, the historical fact that the First London Confession was a reaction against the accusation they were Anabaptists, destroys the idea.

Our interest and discussion now turns to consider the Second London Confession of 1689, the other great particular Baptist confession of the seventeenth century.

CHAPTER 2

THE SECOND LONDON CONFESSION

The next step in our survey of the historical and religious background of the seventeenth century Baptists brings us to the consideration of the Second London Confession. The Backus' publication of the 1646 confession claims that the latter seventeenth century Baptists behind the 1689 confession compromised their convictions as they were forced by the pressure of politics and persecution to use the Westminster Confession as a basis of their new statement of faith. This implies that the Second London Confession was not a correct and adequate representation of particular Baptist theology, especially on the subject of the Law, because they were influenced too much by the Presbyterians.

These are serious accusations against the men behind the 1689 confession. However, the question is, can these accusations be proven? The serious seeker of truth will not be satisfied to read and accept the very brief discussion of another. A conclusion of this sort can only be agreed to if the historical evidence is sufficient. The question of sufficient evidence can only be settled by consideration of the facts of the history surrounding the writing and signing of the 1689 confession of faith. This will be the first task before us in the present chapter, as a brief but factual summary of the political and religious history of England roughly between 1640 and 1689 will be presented.

The Historical Background of the 1689 Confession

The rule of England under Charles I was for the Puritans a disaster. When he came to the throne in 1625, he inherited an uneasy population, and in the passing of the years he did nothing to improve the situation. In fact, with an attitude that many considered to be pompous, he set out to suppress the Puritans, on the one hand, and to force uniformity of religion on the other. He ruled with abandon, ignoring and antagonizing Parliament, and he was fully supported by the Archbishop of Canterbury, William Laud. It should come as no surprise to read that civil war erupted in 1642, and did not end till 1646. The army of Parliament under the leadership of Oliver Cromwell emerged as victors, and opposition to Charles climaxed as he was executed in 1649. Cromwell then ruled England as Lord Protector until 1658.

A portion of the years just discussed above (1640-1648) could be termed the period of Presbyterian Supremacy. During these years they were the ruling power as they controlled Parliament. They immediately proceeded to reform the Church of England. The only problem for Baptists was that the Presbyterians were as opposed to dissent and religious freedom as had been the Anglicans. They too sought to establish a state church. When the Westminster Assembly convened in 1643 Baptists were excluded. Not only were they excluded, but they were also misunderstood and falsely accused by the Presbyterians. It was out of this atmosphere of misrepresentation and false accusation that Baptists published the First London Confession in 1644.

The rule of Cromwell was probably a relief for Baptists, for he was a religious man, and even though he stood for a state church, he at least desired some measure of religious toleration. Perhaps he even established in England the greatest amount of religious liberty it had ever experienced up to that hour of its history. However the contending forces and the differing convictions were too strong for religious toleration and liberty to last. When Cromwell retired in 1659 and was replaced by his son, the Church of England soon vaulted to power once again. As Richard Cromwell was unable to sustain the rule of his father, Charles II was able to come to the throne, and with the Church of England also reestablished the persecution and jailing of Dissenters (Baptists included). In the years that followed ecclesiastical laws against the Dissenters abounded.

In 1661 Charles issued a proclamation which prohibited the gathering of unlawful and seditious meetings under the pretense of religious worship. A series of acts issued from 1661-1665 known as the *Clarendon Code* further and completely devastated Presbyterianism of any strength that may have remained. Understandably, the acts also brought hardship and difficulty to Baptists. The *Corporation Act* of 1661 resulted in removing Baptists and other Dissenters from activity in societal life.

In 1662 the *Act of Uniformity* was passed, and, as the title states, sought to force a uniformity in religious life upon all. It required full agreement with the articles of the Church of England and the Book of Common Prayer by all ministers. This led to the exclusion of Presbyterian, Baptist, and Congregational pastors from their churches. What a strange reversal this was. The Presbyterians, having gone from the persecuted to the persecutors, now became the persecuted once again right alongside of the Baptists and others they had persecuted. Now they were both Dissenters who were opposed by the State Church, and further, they were both considered sects by the ruling Church.

In 1664 the *Conventicle Act* was passed, and it prohibited any one over six years old from being present at any worship service other than the ones authorized by the Church of England. The penalty for this alleged crime was imprisonment for the first two offenses. On the third offense, one was banished to America for a period of years. Appeal wasn't even a possibility for the offender.

In 1665 the *Five-Mile Act* was published, which was a law requiring nonconformist preachers to swear an oath that they would not rebel or practice sedition against the king, his officers, or government. The penalty for breaking this law was virtually exile from the cities.

In 1670 the *Second Conventicle Act* was passed, and this law gave authorities the power to arrest unlawful worshipers. It also brought a heavy fine to the minister, the worshipers, and the owner of the building where they met. The success of this law was virtually guaranteed in light of the fact the informer in the situation was rewarded one third of the fine.

In 1672 there was some rest from persecution brought by the *Declaration of Indulgence*. Issued by Charles, it removed all ecclesiastical laws against Dissenters, including Roman Catholics. This edict led to the release of many from prison, including John Bunyan, who had languished for twelve years in confinement. Thus, after twelve years (1660-1672) of heavy persecution, the Dissenters had some hope, a measure of toleration and freedom, and were able to worship how and where they desired.

In 1673 this measure of freedom and toleration ended as Parliament forced Charles to withdraw the *Declaration of Indulgence*. They then passed the *Test Act*, and persecution fell on Dissenters again. John Bunyan returned at this point to prison once again also. This burst of strong and renewed persecution did bring Baptists and Presbyterians closer together. It is true that Baptists at this juncture were desirous to show a unified spirit with other various groups of Dissenters. It is true also that part of the result of this desire was the writing or drawing up of the Second London Confession in 1677. It must be remembered, however, that it was not signed until 1689. Further, it is also true that this confession used a non-Baptist source—the Westminster Confession of Faith (remember here that the First London Confession had used non-Baptist sources also). On the other hand, there is not one shred of historical evidence that anyone or any group of anything forced these Baptists to use the Westminster Confession as a basis. Where is there to be found a single statement or even a single intimation by the men of that day (Baptists or their opponents) or from historians who followed (again Baptists or their opponents) that these Baptists were forced to use the Westminster Confession? These men were not the average twentieth-century Baptists who would probably fold and fade away at the first threat of persecution. These Baptists of the seventeenth century were reared and steeped in a background of persecution, as the above historical survey evidences. It is impossible to believe and even ridiculous to suggest that these honorable men of conviction, who had suffered so much in the past, and who were suffering as much in the present, would cave-in to the pressure of persecution and therefore compromise their doctrinal position. Such a suggestion or thought is only the assumption of some moderns who read and then rewrite history on the basis of their own imagination in hope of justifying a doctrinal conviction they have already subjectively embraced. The evidence does not support any contention that Baptists of this period consciously or unconsciously succumbed to force as they used the Westminster Confession as a basis for the Second London Confession.

To continue the historical survey, it is to be noted that in 1685 James II, a Roman Catholic, came to the throne. Several attempts were made against his rule, but these failed, and the leaders and some participants in the rebellions were executed. Persecution broke out again in a heavy and severe manner, perhaps as fierce as at any time previously. Many persons were either imprisoned or executed because of dissent. But these stringent conditions ceased once again in April of 1687 as James issued the *Declaration of Indulgence*. This act emptied the jails, ended the persecution, and brought other relief to the Dissenters.

Finally in 1689 the *Toleration Act* was enacted under the reign of Mary, the Protestant daughter of James, and her husband, William of Orange. It is to be noted that the particular Baptists met in 1689 and signed the Second London Confession after the passing of the *Toleration Act*. This is an important point which is to be further pursued under the next heading.

The Act of Toleration

In the previous section of this chapter the historical and religious background of the Second London Confession was traced. The years up to 1689 were mostly years of persecution for Baptists, except for a few years of respite at several intervals. It was pointed out that the Second London Confession was written in 1677, and that though it used the Westminster Confession as a source, there is no evidence whatsoever that it was from any motive of force. What about the signing of the Confession of 1689. Was it from a voluntary motive, or was it from compulsion?

Again, as before, the evidence will only sustain the conclusion that these Baptists of 1689 signed the confession voluntarily. Remember, first, that James II had issued the *Declaration of Indulgence* in 1687, two years prior to the signing of the confession. This law was a break-through and freed many religious prisoners. But even further than this law was the passing of the *Act of Toleration*, and what did it do?

Perhaps the best way to inform the reader of some of the details of this law will be to quote respected historians concerning its importance, provisions, and results. Note the following testimonies:

> For the modern historian, as he looks back over the far stretch of Nonconformist history from Nonconformity's first appearance until now, can find no moment of time which so definitely marks a new epoch in that history as does the Toleration Act of 1689. Whether or no the new opportunities which then descended upon Nonconformity were wisely used, it is certain that new opportunities did descend: whether or no the Nonconformity fully recognised the new responsibilities, as well as new privileges, which henceforth rested upon it, it is certain that both new privileges and new responsibilities were sent; and however many the remaining adversaries without and within may have been, and however sadly to some of them Nonconformity may have succumbed, it is certain that to Nonconformity there was opened a great and effectual door. For the Toleration Act signalized the close of Nonconformity's long struggle for existence, and conferred upon it in perpetuity the right to be.[1]

> The Act of Toleration, designed to give 'Some ease to scrupulous consciences in the exercise of religion,' was grudgingly granted to Presbyterians, Independents, Baptists, and Quakers, because persecution had utterly failed to accomplish its object. The absurdity and uselessness, though not the impiety and injustice, or attempting to coerce conscience had been demonstrated. To lash the entire people into the use of one fixed form of creed and ritual was seen to be impossible. Hence a slight concession was wrung from the dominant party, impelled by a necessity from which there was no escape.[2]

The Toleration Act of 1689 brought to an end the persecution to which Nonconformists has been subject at intervals and in periods of varying intensity since the restoration. Writing more that a century and half later, Macaulay ranked it as 'among those great statutes which are epochs in our constitutional history' and this remains true. The Act guarantees freedom of worship to those who dissent from the forms and ceremonies of the Church of England.[3]

After 1689 they were given a measure of toleration such as they had never known in England—since it was toleration secured and clearly defined by law, not given by the arbitrary will of one man.[4]

As we have already observed the spirit of toleration towards Dissenters had been at work long before the Toleration Act of 1689. Comprehension as a principle had been found unworkable. The Act of Uniformity had completely failed to produce uniformity and extinguish dissent. The Nonconformist not only remained irreconcilable and unsubdued, but at the end of the twenty-five years were more numerous than ever. Such a situation could not remain unobserved. A growing respect for Dissenters; a recognition of the fact that they represented an important group of citizens of value in the emerging political party-system; the economic necessity of preserving useful members of the community in the interests of national prosperity; the recognition that truth cannot be the exclusive possession of one side; the greater understanding of the claims of reason—all these factors acted as solvent forces upon the idea that persecution of men for religion was a justifiable procedure.[5]

The above statements must not be interpreted as indicating that England in this period of its history now became the possessor of full religious freedom. The next set of quotations will show that though the *Toleration Act* was a real turn in the right direction, it did not give full religious liberty.

> It will be seen that the toleration thus granted by the Act was limited and conditional. There was a certain admission of the rights of conscience in matters of worship, but freedom of civil status was not granted. It still remained impossible for Nonconformists to hold office under the Crown or in civil life, and universities remained closed against them.[6]

> This Act, which subsequently received the popular title of 'Toleration Act,' gave as may be supposed from the temper of the times in which it passed, the smallest possible advantage to the Dissenters from the established religion. The only dissent which it recognized or allowed was dissent from forms and ceremonies; it allowed none from the established doctrines of the Church. The preamble recited that its object was to give some ease to scrupulous consciences, in order that Protestants might be more united in interest and affection.[7]

> It should be carefully noticed that the Toleration Act did not repeal the persecuting laws; it merely granted exemption from them to such persons as should fulfill certain prescribed conditions. It was not a concession of the principle of religious freedom (which indeed by implication it definitely disclaimed), but merely a recognition of the fact that, within certain limits, religious dissent did not imply hostility to the state or to the social order. It was the outcome of political exigency, not of reverence for the rights of the individual conscience.[8]

> This Act of Toleration, be it observed, was not a literal repeal of the Clarendon Code. There was nothing in it to give hope to any who still looked for a Calvinist and Presbyterian Church of England. It was in part a

rationalizing and civilizing of much that had already taken place. It provided, to be precise, for the repeal of the ancient Elizabethan order that made it legal to levy fines on Dissenters for failure to attend their parish church, and for the withdrawal of all power to prosecute Dissenters, whether Protestant or Catholic, merely for their dissent. But it did not in so many words declare the Corporation Act, the Act of Uniformity, the Conventicle Acts, the Five Mile Act and the Test Act void; nor did it remove from Dissenters those political and social disabilities which the Clarendon Code had laid on them.[9]

The Toleration Act passed in 1689 was anomalous; but at least it brought to an end the active persecution of Dissenters and accepted them as an element likely to be permanent and entitled to some recognition. It may be said to have involved toleration but not full liberty of conscience, much less real religious equality. It did not allow dissent from the accepted doctrinal standards of the Church. Nor did Dissenters at first desire this, though a few among them already objected to the principle of subscription... The Anglican Church continued as the Established Church, and religious tests remained for public offices. Nevertheless Nonconformists were granted the right to worship in their own way, although they had to register their meeting-houses and were subject to a number of older restrictions.[10]

Therefore we must conclude that the Act of Toleration was limited and did not grant full religious freedom and liberty. There were still laws against Dissenters on the books, but, nevertheless, one should not underestimate the significance of this act, and the measure of freedom and toleration it brought, especially in light of what the Nonconformists had faced in the past. The positive results of the act can be seen in the following statements:

Such as it was, then, with all its incompleteness, the Toleration Act marked a momentous advance towards that religious liberty so ably advocated in Locke's 'Epistola de Tolerantia,' which appeared a few months later in an English translation.[11]

...generally speaking the Nonconformists readily took advantage of the Act of Toleration. Nearly one thousand chapels were built within the twenty years that followed, the majority being Presbyterian, the Baptists probably coming next in number, and the independents a good third.[12]

During the last quarter of the seventeenth century, the number of Nonconformists may be fairly estimated at more than 150,000 and probably nearer 250,000 in addition to which were the Quakers. The last years of the century witnessed the consolidation of Nonconformity.[13]

The Toleration Act of 1689 had confirmed the Anglican Church in power but had given some limited recognition to Dissenters. Both parties therefore enjoyed a measure of prosperity...[14]

...the spirit of the Toleration Act was practiced much more widely than the letter warranted.[15]

The reader may wonder what constitutes the point of all this discussion of the *Act of Toleration*. It has become an important issue because some modern Baptists have claimed these Baptists of the latter part of the seventeenth century compromised their convictions as they were pressured by the political and religious circumstances of the day. This is the only reason some can see for their using the Westminster Confession as a basis for their Second London Confession. It has already been stated that there is not one shred of evidence that this was the case when the confession was originally drawn up in 1677. Yet even further the evidence is strong against such a possibility when one considers the official signing of the confession. The fact is that the *Toleration Act* was passed on May 24, 1689, while the Second London Confession was signed in early July of the same year.

This means that the pressure was off Baptists when they signed the Second London Confession. The *Act of Toleration* had been passed almost two months previously. Even if they had been under pressure when the confession was written in 1677, and if they had compromised their convictions then, there was no pressure when they signed the confession. One must conclude with Payne, the well respected English Baptist scholar that 'These seventeenth century confessions give clear expressions to the convictions of the early Baptists.'[16] With this conclusion, William Lumpkin, the respected American Baptist historian agrees, as he stated, 'Essential agreement with the London Confession of 1644 was claimed in the introductory note, but scarcity of copies and general ignorance of that Confession, as well as the need for more full and distinct expression of voices than the Confession offered, were given as reasons for preparing the new Confession.'[17] Notice that Lumpkin does not give political or religious pressure as a reason for the Second London Confession. He also believes that Baptists in 1689 believed very strongly what they signed in that confession.[18]

Why the Westminster Confession?

If the authors and signers of the Second London Confession did not use the confession because of pressure, how can one explain their reason for using it as the basic source of a Baptist confession of faith? Several reasons can be suggested for this action.

First, it was a common practice in that day. Religious groups, setting forth their doctrinal convictions often used an earlier confession, and it did not have to be one of their particular denomination. Remember that the 1644 confession used several earlier non-Baptist sources.

Second, the Westminster Confession is an excellent statement of Calvinistic faith, and was well-suited to their purposes as these particular Baptists were also strong Calvinists. In fact the Westminster standard, having stood the test of time, is probably now the most respected and famous of Calvinistic confessions. It should be obvious that these particular Baptists of the seventeenth century showed sound judgment in recognizing the Westminster Confession as a superior standard at this young stage of that confession's history. How foolish they would have been to write their own statement from the ground up when such a standard as the Westminster Confession was available. In simple words, it was wisdom for them to use the Westminster Standard as a basis for a new Baptist statement of faith.

Third, another reason for using the Westminster Confession was that it would give anyone who wished to check a ready reference as to what Baptists believed. One already familiar with the Westminster Confession would quickly see the agreements and the disagreement between Presbyterians and Baptists. The agreements were greater in number, but there were places Baptists changed certain sections that would have violated their convictions concerning church, ministry, and sacraments.[19] It should be obvious to the reader at this point too that if Baptists refused to receive the entire Westminster Confession, but changed it at places where there was disagreement, then if the statement on the Law of God was not a particular Baptist conviction, they would have changed it also. One might argue that these Baptists did not state particular Baptist thought *if* they had adopted the entire Westminster Confession. Or again, one could argue that point *if* even one clear Baptist doctrine had been violated in their use of the Westminster Confession as a basis. But there is no argument when Baptists clearly changed just those points and all those points which obviously violated Baptist doctrine.

Other Arguments

Briefly, several other arguments need to be stated which defeat the current contention that the First and Second London Confessions have different views of the Law.

First, the preface to the Second London Confession sees this new statement as a continuation and expansion of the 1644 confession rather than a contradiction or correction.[20] In these pages they speak of a difference in their new confession in method and manner of expression, but quickly state that 'the substance of the matter is the same.'[21] To accuse the First and Second London Confessions of having different views of the Law, is to accuse the men who wrote the preface to the latter of being either dishonest or ignorant. Surely these men were honest men, and surely they knew more about these two confessions than twentieth century Baptists. Therefore, the preface is clear evidence that both London Confessions have the same view of the Law.

Second, the fact that William Kiffen signed both confessions is strong evidence they do not have a contradiction on the subject of the Law.[22] The only other possibility is that Kiffen changed his view, but where is the evidence of this? Rather, Kiffen attested his signature to both the First and Second London Confessions of Faith because he saw them both as adequate expressions of particular Baptist faith with no distinction on the subject of the Law. Another Baptist of this era, Hanserd Knollys, signed both the 1646 edition and the Second London Confession of 1689.[23] If one wonders why other signers of the First London Confession did not pen the Second, the answer is two-fold. On the one hand, there were only fifteen signatures to the early confession, which does limit the candidates for the task. On the other hand, forty-five years transpired between the two confessions. Most of the original penmen of the 1644 confession were probably dead by 1689. Kiffen was twenty-eight years old in 1644 and may well have been the youngest signature on the early confession. This means he was seventy-three when he signed the 1689 confession. Knolly was forty-eight years old when he signed the 1646 edition, but then lived till 1691. He died at the age of ninety-three, thus being enabled also to sign the 1689 confession.[24] This is strong evidence these confessions were in agreement with no differing views of the Law.

Summary

The arguments of this chapter are complete. It has been shown that it is a fallacious argument to maintain that the First and Second London Confessions have differing views of the Law of God. This opinion must be rejected for the following reasons:

1. The historical background of the 1689 confession shows it was not forced on Baptists as some are claiming (which would account for a supposed different view of the Law), but rather it was a voluntary statement which set forth a particular Baptist view of the Law which was in agreement with the 1644 confession.

2. The Toleration Act was signed in 1689 before the Second London Confession was signed. When Baptists signed this later confession, they acted therefore voluntarily and not from political pressure.

3. The authors of the 1689 confession used the Westminster Confession as the basis for their doctrinal statement not because they were forced to do so, but, among other reasons, because it was a Calvinistic confession and it was a common practice of the day. Political factors did encourage them to stand with the Presbyterians, but it was not a coerced or a forced decision.

4. The best Baptist historians of England and the United States of the past and present see no compulsion in the authorship of and attestment to the Second London Confession, nor do they see a distinction in the doctrine of the law between the early and later confessions.

5. The authors of the Second London Confession changed considerable statements of the Westminster Confession, which was their basis in writing. They freely changed non-Baptist views, and would have changed the statement on the Law had it truly not been a particular Baptist conviction and in disagreement with the First London Confession.

6. The preface to the Second London Confession of Faith sees the views expressed therein as a continuation and expansion of the First London Confession rather than a contradiction of it at any point. There is an acknowledgement of a difference of method and manner of expression, but also a claim that the substance of the confession is the same.

7. William Kiffen signed both the First and Second London Confessions, which is a testimony of the

fact they carried the same doctrinal convictions. This testimony is strengthened when one notes also that Hanserd Knollys also signed the 1646 edition and the 1689 confession.

CONCLUSION

It is not the purpose of this section to summarize or even restate the arguments or conclusions of the previous chapters. If one wishes to survey the ideas of those chapters, a summary is provided at the end of each. Rather, the purpose for this conclusion is to make several critical observations concerning modern Baptists who are advocating a New Covenant emphasis of the Law to the exclusion of the Old Covenant statement of the Law of God. What is said here (as in the rest of this work) is spoken in love. We have deep respect for the men who are advocating these views, but we feel compelled to speak against their theology and methods. We are in no way questioning their salvation or sincerity, but we must make several critical observations concerning the entire scene as it has and is developing before us.

First, it should be clear by now that their position is based on a very shoddy and unjustified handling of the historical facts. They have read history and interpreted it only to justify their convictions. They have made statements and drawn from those statements unjustified conclusions. They have pointed out some historical facts and then jumped premises and other historical facts to arrive at their desired convictions. They have magnified some facts of history and drawn conclusions from them, while ignoring others that would have contradicted their conclusions. In simple words, they have handled the historical method of research very poorly!

Second, it must be stated that they are leading a great number of others blindly into their convictions. It is a sad thing for a man to mishandle history, but it is sadder yet when one sets himself and his view up as correct and then seeks to lead others in that direction. A false view couched in proper convincing language by a respected man or group of men, even though it ignores pertinent facts, will be believed, because we live in a shallow day and age when most will not check the facts, but rather find it easier to believe the strong statements and arguments of another, even if he is wrong. If anyone reads this manuscript, who has swallowed the reasoning and arguments of the New Covenant men regarding their analysis of the seventeenth century Baptist confessions, our prayer is that such a one will be open to hear the truth of the facts and if not yet convinced as we have presented them, he will go to the historical materials and research the matter for himself. Much more is at stake, my brother, than just you as you have listened to the weak arguments of another. At stake are the ones you will teach, and the ones they will teach, and the ones to be taught for generations to come. This is a serious subject and one must not allow himself to be swept into a new viewpoint simply because someone of standing and persuasion promotes it.

Third, the New Covenant men would be more consistent to align themselves historically with Anabaptists than with the particular Baptists of seventeenth century England. Why try to re-write or re-interpret the seventeenth century particular Baptist confessions, when actually they have already an historical basis for their views in the Anabaptists? Why make the early Particular Baptists say things they never really said, or believe things they never really believed? If these New Covenant men so strongly desire to show their view has historical roots, let them use the real groups that mirror their convictions, particularly many of the Anabaptists.

Fourth, the New Covenant men would, if they do not wish to align themselves historically with the Anabaptists on this issue, be more respected if they sought to argue their views from Scripture alone. This certainly is not to say Scripture teaches their view. But it is to say, that if one finds he is no longer in agreement with a confession that he has cherished for some time because he thinks it is in disagreement with Scripture, he would do best to affirm he disagrees with and rejects that confession in preference to what he believes Scripture teaches. He should not force that confession to agree with his new viewpoint. It is rumored that these men of the New Covenant view are planning a new confession of their own in the future. This too would be more respectable than seeking to twist an old confession to make it agree with their new view.

Fifth, and finally, the New Covenant men, by their shoddy handling of history, have raised a definite question as to their ability to handle Scripture as well. Can ones who have read their own convictions into the historical record by such poor use of the historical method and by such a shallow reading of the historical material be trusted to guide us in such a deep theological study as it is found in Scripture? Yes, the subject of the Law of God is a deep theological subject! No one can deny that! One cannot understand this subject by a shallow and surface approach to Scripture. One cannot understand this subject by proof-texting a few verses of Scripture. One cannot understand this subject by a supposed in-depth study of one or two passages of Scripture. One should not be persuaded to a position on this subject by shrewd sophistry. One can only understand this subject by a careful handling of God's Word. One who has handled history so shabbily is suspect when he then also claims he can handle Scripture in such a difficult area. If one allows

personal prejudice or personal conviction to rule his historical interpretations, what guarantee is there that the same will
not be true as he seeks to interpret Scripture?

These are our final conclusions. Be reminded that this
work is not sent forth of our own initiative. It is a necessity
for us to write these words because others have
misinterpreted history on a key subject of theology, and we
cannot remain silent. We do not contend that the issue is
settled simply because we have shown the true understanding of the seventeenth century particular Baptists concerning the Law of God. The final authority, we do
acknowledge, is the Word of God. We have shown the two
London Confessions do not have a New Covenant emphasis
of the Law of God, as some are contending today. The real
question remains—what does the Scripture teach? Perhaps
in the future we may address that question in writing also.
But for now our task is finished.

Endnotes

Introduction

1. Gary D. Long, 'Contemporary Preface' to *A Confession of Faith* (Rochester, NY: Backus Publishers, 1981).

2. Ibid., pp. iii-iv.

3. Ibid., back cover.

4. Ibid., p. vi.

Chapter 1

1. W. J. McGlothlin, *Baptist Confessions of Faith* (Philadelphia: American Baptist Publicaton Society, 1911), p. 169.

2. W. T. Whitley, *A History of British Baptists* (London: The Kingsgate Press, 1932), p. 89.

3. Ibid.

4. W. J. McGlothlin, 'The Sources of the First Calvinistic Baptist Confession of Faith,'*Review and Expositor* (Vol. XIII, 4, October 1916), pp. 502-505.

5. Robert B. Hannen, 'A Suggested Source of Some Expressions in the Baptist Confessions of Faith, London 1644,' *The Baptist Quarterly* (Vol. XII, 1946-1949), pp. 390-395.

6. McGlothlin, 'The Sources,' p. 502.

7. Ibid.

8. Ibid.

9. Ibid.

10. Ibid.

11. Ibid.

12. McGlothlin, *Baptist Confessions*, p. 169.

13. *A Confession of Faith*, cover page.

14. W. J. McGlothlin, 'Featley and the First Calvinistic Baptist Confession,' *Review and Expositor* (Vol. VI, 4, 1909), p. 582.

15. Ibid., p. 588.

16. McGlothlin, *Baptist Confessions*, p. 190.

17. Ibid.

18. McGlothlin, 'Featley,' pp. 587-588.

19. Ibid, p. 587.

20. Ibid.

21. Ibid., p. 588.

22. Ibid.

23. Ibid.

24. McGlothlin, 'Sources,' p. 589.

25. See also William L. Lumpkin, *Baptist Confessions of Faith* (Philadelphia: The Judson Press, 1959), p. 147. Lumpkin agrees with McGlothlin as he says also, '...much of the distinctly Baptist emphasis was removed from some of the articles.'

26. It is quite interesting that when Gary Long quotes a paragraph that begins by mentioning changes in the 1646 confession due to Featley's criticism, he deletes that part, and quotes only section of the paragraph which is favorable to the 1646 confession. This may be unintentional, but nonetheless it looks suspicious. See *A Confession of Faith*, p. vi and compare to Lumpkin, *Baptist Confessions*, p. 148.

27. Lumpkin, *Baptist Confessions*, p. 148.

28. *A Baptist Confession*, p. 23.

29. Ibid.

30. McGlothlin, *Baptist Confessions*, p. 195.

31. Ibid.

32. Whitley, *A History of Baptists*, pp. 94-95.

33. Ibid.

34. Ibid.

35. Ibid.

36. Ibid.

37. *A Baptist Confession of Faith*, pp. iii-iv.

38. Ibid., p. 4.

39. Ibid., p. 11.

40. Ibid.

41. Ibid., p. 14.

42. Ibid., p. 17.

43. Ibid., p. 20.

44. Ibid., p. 3.

45. Ibid., p. 16.

46. Ibid., p. 18.

47. William L. Lumpkin, telephone interview, September 16, 1982.

48. *A Confession of Faith*, title page.

49. Ibid., cover page.

50. William Klassen, 'The Relationship of the Old and New Covenants in Pilgram Marpeck's Theology,' *Mennonite Quarterly Review* (Vol XL, 2, April 1966), p. 97.

51. William Estep, *The Anabaptist Story* (Grand Rapids: Eerdmans Publishing Company, 1963), pp. 142-143.

Chapter 2

1. Henry W. Clark, *History of English Nonconformity*, Vol. II (New York: Russell and Russell, 1965), p. 119.

2. Eri B. Hulbert, *The English Reformation and Puritanism*, edited by Are Wyant (Chicago: University of Chicago Press, 1908), pp. 330-331.

3. E. A. Payne, 'Toleration and Establishment,' *From Uniformity to Unity* 1662-1962, edited by Geoffrey F. Nuttall and Chadwick Owen (London: 1952), pp. 258-259.

4. Henry Vedder, *A Short History of Baptists* (Valley Forge: The Judson Press, 1978), p. 237.

5. John T. Wilkinson, *1662—and After* (London: Epworth Press, 1962), p. 98.

6. Ibid., p. 101.

7. Herbert S. Skeats, *History of the Free Church of England* (London: James Clark and Co., 1891), p. 104.

8. A. A. Seaton, *The Theory of Toleration Under the Later Stuarts* (New York: Octagon Books, 1972), p. 233.

9. Erik Routley, *English Religious Dissent* (London: Cambridge University Press, 1960), p. 124.

10. E. A. Payne, *The Free Church in the Life of England* (London: SCM Press, 1951), p. 59.

11. Seaton, *The Theory of Toleration*, p. 236.

12. Wilkinson, *1662—and After*, p. 103.

13. Ibid., pp. 102-103.

14. Payne, *The Free Church*, p. 69.

15. Ibid., p. 59-60.

16. E. A. Payne, *The Fellowhsip of Believers* (London: The Carey Kingsgate Press, 1952), p. 76.

17. William L. Lumpkin, *Baptist Confessions of Faith* (Philadelphia: The Judson Press, 1959), p. 237.

18. William L. Lumpkin, telephone interview, September 16, 1982.

19. W. T. Whitley, *A History of British Baptists* (London: The Kingsgate Press, 1932), pp. 128-129.

20. Lumpkin, *Baptist Confessions*, pp. 244-248.

21. Ibid., p. 244.

22. W. T. Whitley, 'The Seven Churches of London,' *Review and Expositor*, Vol. VII, July 1910, 3 (Louisville, KY: The Seminary Press), p. 393. See also John C. Carlile, *The Story of English Baptists* (London: James Clarke and Co., 1905), p. 87. See also McGlothlin, *Baptist Confessions*, p. 174.

23. Whitley, 'Seven Churches,' p. 396.

24. Lumpkin, *Baptist Confessions*, p. 171.

BIBLIOGRAPHY

Armitage, Thomas. *The History of Baptists*. Chicago:
    Morningside Publishing Company, 1887.

Carlile, J. C. *The Story of English Baptists*. London: James Clarke
    and Company, 1905.

Christian, John T. *A History of the Baptists*. Nashville: Broadman
    Press, 1922.

Clark, Henry W. *History of English Nonconformity*. Vol. II. New
    York: Russell and Russell, 1965.

A Confession of Faith. Rochester, NY: Backus Books, 1981.

Cook, Richard B. *The Story of Baptists*. Greenwood, SC: The Attic
    Press, Inc., 1973.

Cooper, Duncan. *English Dissent Under the Early Hanorerians*.
    London: The Epworth Press, 1946.

Curtis, George Herbert. *Dissent in its Relation to the Church of
    England*. London: MacMillian and Company, 1873.

Dosker, Henery Elias. *The Dutch Anabaptists*. Philadelphia:
    Judson Press, 1921.

Estep, William. *The Anabaptist Story*. Grand Rapids: Eerdmans
    Publishing Company, 1963.

Hannen, Robert B. "A Suggested Source of Some Expressions in the Baptist Confession of Faith, London 1644." *The Baptist Quarterly*, XII, 1946-1949.

Heishberger, Guy. "Book Review." *Mennonite Quarterly Review*. XVII, January 1943.

Hulbert, Eri B. *The English Reformation and Puritianism*. Edited by Are Wyant. Chicago: University of Chicago Press, 1908.

Klassen, William. "The Relationship of the Old and New Covenants in Pilgram Marpeck's Theology." *Mennonite Quarter ly Review*, XL, 2, April 1966.

Latourette, Kenneth Scott. *A History of Christianity*. New York: Harper and Row, 1953.

Lumpkin, William L. *Baptist Confessions of Faith*. Philadelphia: The Judson Press, 1959.

McGlothlin, W. J. *Baptist Confessions of Faith*. Philadelphia: American Baptist Publication Society, 1911.

_____. "Featley and the First Calvinistic Baptist Confession." *Review and Expositor*, Vol. VI, 4, 1909.

_____. "Sources of the First Calvinistic Baptist Confession of Faith." Vol. XIII, 4, October 1916.

Nuttall, Geoffery F. and Chadwick, Owen, editors. *From Uniformity to Unity 1662-1962*, London: 1952.

Payne, Earnest A. *The Fellowhsip of Believers*. London: The Carey Kingsgate Press, 1952.

_____. *The Free Church Tradition in the Life of England*. London: SCM Press, 1951.

Routley, Erik. *English Religious Dissent*. London: Cambridge University Press, 1960.

Seaton, A. A. *The Theory of Toleration Under the Later Stuarts*. New York: Octagon Books, 1972.

Skeats, Herbert S. *History of the Free Church of England*. London: James Clarke and Company, 1981.

Stevenson, William. *The Story of the Reformation*. Richmond: John Knox Press, 1959.

Torbet, Robert. *A History of the Baptists*. Philadelphia: The Judson Press, 1950.

Underwood, A. C. *A History of the English Baptists*. London: The Carey Kingsgate Press Limited, 1st Printing, 1947. Second Printing, 1961.

Vedder, Henry. *A Short History of the Baptists*. Valley Forge: The Judson Press, 1978.

Whiting, C. E. *Studies in English Puritanism from the Restoration to the Revolution 1660-1688*. New York and Toronto: MacMillian and Company, 1931.

Whitley, W. T. *A History of British Baptists*. London: The Kingsgate Press, 1932.

_____. "The Seven Churches of London." *Review and Expositor*, Vol. VII, 3, July 1910.

Wilkinson, John T. *1662—And After.* London: Epworth Press, 1962.